1936

THE LAMP
AND THE BELL

THE LAMP
AND THE BELL

A DRAMA IN FIVE ACTS

BY

EDNA ST. VINCENT MILLAY

Publishers
HARPER & BROTHERS
NEW YORK AND LONDON

THE LAMP AND THE BELL

A DRAMA IN FIVE ACTS

By EDNA ST. VINCENT MILLAY

Written on the occasion of the Fiftieth Anniversary of the Founding of the Vassar College Alumnæ Association

Dedicated to "1917"

LORENZO, King of Fiori

MARIO, King of Lagoverde

GUIDO, Duke of Versilia, illegitimate nephew to Lorenzo

GIOVANNI
LUIGI
ANSELMO
RAFFAELE
} Gentlemen at the court of Lorenzo

FIDELIO, Jester at the court of Lorenzo

GIUSEPPE, Agent for the Duke's estates

CESCO
HORATIO
} Townsmen of Fiori

BEPPO, a little boy, son to GIULIANA

RIGO, little boy, son to LEONORA

CLERK

MESSENGER

OCTAVIA, Lorenzo's second wife

BEATRICE, "Rose-Red," Daughter to Lorenzo by a former marriage

BIANCA, "Snow-White," Daughter to Octavia by a former marriage

CAST OF CHARACTERS

LAURA
CARLOTTA
FRANCESCA
VIOLA
LILINA
LELA } Ladies at the court of Lorenzo
ARIANNA
CLAUDIA
CLARA
LUCIA

GRAZIA, Nurse to Beatrice and Bianca
GIULIETTA, Servant to Bianca
"LITTLE SNOW-WHITE"
"LITTLE ROSE-RED"

LEONORA
GIULIANA
CLARA } Women of Fiori
GIOVANITTA
ANNA
EUGENIA

ELEANORA
LUISA } little girls, daughters to Leonora

GILDA, a little girl, sister to Beppo
ADELINA, another little girl
NURSE

PIERROT
HARLEQUIN
PANTALOON } Strolling players
POLICHINELLO
COLOMBINE

*Courtiers, Ladies-in-Waiting, Soldiers, Pages,
Musicians, Townspeople, Children*

THE LAMP
AND THE BELL

THE LAMP AND THE BELL

PROLOGUE

[Anselmo and Luigi]

ANSELMO.   What think you, — lies there any
 truth in the tale
The King will wed again?

LUIGI.   Why not, Anselmo?
A king is no less lonely than a collier
When his wife dies. And his young daughter there,
For all her being a princess, is no less
A motherless child, and cries herself to sleep
Night after night, as noisily as any,
You may be sure.

ANSELMO. A motherless child loves not,
They say, the second mother. Though the King
May find him comfort in another face, —
As it is well he should — the child, I fancy,
Is not so lonely as she is distraught
With grief for the dead Queen, and will not lightly
Be parted from her tears.

LUIGI.   If tales be true,
The woman hath a daughter, near the age
Of his, will be a playmate for the Princess.

CURTAIN

ACT I

Scene 1

A garden of the palace at Fiori; four years later.

Discovered seated Laura, Francesca and Fidelio, Laura embroidering, Fidelio strumming his flute, Francesca lost in thought.

LAURA. You — Fool! If there be two chords to your lute,

Give us the other for a time!

FRANCESCA.   And yet, Laura,
I somewhat fancied that soft sound he made.
'Twas all on the same tone, — but 'twas a sweet tone.

LAURA. 'Tis like you. As for myself, let music change

From time to time, or have done altogether.
Sing us the song, Fidelio, that you made
Last night, — a song of flowers, and fair skies,

And nightingales, and love.

FIDELIO.   I know the song.
It is a song of winter.

LAURA.   How is that?

FIDELIO. Because it is a song of summer set
To a sad tune.

FRANCESCA (*sadly*). Ah, well, — so that it be not
A song of autumn, I can bear to hear it.

LAURA. In any case, music. I am in a mood for music.
I am in a mood where if something be not done
To startle me, I shall confess my sins.
[*Enter Carlotta.*

CARLOTTA. Ha! I will have that woman yet by the
hair!

LAURA. What woman, pray, Carlotta?

CARLOTTA.   Ho! What woman?
Who but that scullery-wench, that onion-monger,
That slatternly, pale bakeress, that foul witch,
The coroneted Fishwife of Fiori,
Her Majesty, the Queen!

FRANCESCA.   Hush — hush — Carlotta!
You could be put to death for less than that!

CARLOTTA. Not I, my duck. When I am put to death
'Twill be for more! Oh, I will have her yet

By the hair! (*For the first time noticing Fidelio*)
     Fidelio, if you breathe one word
Of this, I will scratch the Princess into ribbons,
Whom you love better than your wit.

FIDELIO.   I' faith,
I did but hear you say you are a fishwife,
And all the world knows that.

LAURA.   Fear not, Carlotta,
He is as dumb as a prophet. Every second word
He utters eats the one before it. Speak,
But softly.

CARLOTTA. Nay, 'tis nothing. — Nay, by my head,
It is a townful! 'Tis the way she has
Of saying "That should be done like this, and this
Like that"! The woman stirs me to that point
I feel like a carrot in a stew, — I boil so
I bump the kettle on all sides!

LAURA.   My dear,
Were you as plump as I you would not dare
Become so angry. It would make your stays creak.

CARLOTTA. Well, I am done. Fidelio, play me a dirge
To put me in good spirits. Merry music
Is sure to make me sad.

(*Fidelio plays. Pause.*)

'Tis curious
A woman like her should have a child like that —
So gentle and so pretty-mannered.   Faith, —

FIDELIO.   Hush! Hush! Here come the prettiest pair
of birds
That ever sat together on a bough so close
You could not see the sky between.   How now,
Snow-White and Rose-Red! Are you reconciled
One to another?

[*Enter Beatrice and Bianca, with their arms about
each other.*

BIANCA.   Reconciled, Fidelio?
We had not quarreled!

[*Laughter from Fidelio and the ladies.*

BEATRICE.   Do not listen to him,
Bianca, 'tis but the jingling of his bells.
Fidelio, do you make a better jest than that
At once, or have the clappers cut from them.

FIDELIO.   Alas, alas, — all the good jests are made.
I made them yesterday.

CARLOTTA.   If that be true,
You would best become a wise man for a time,
My friend, — there are plenty of wise words not yet
said!

FIDELIO. I shall say them all to-morrow.

LAURA. If you do,
You will be stoned to death.

FIDELIO. Not I. No one
Will hear me. — Well, I am off. — I know an old man
Who does not know the road runs past his house;
And yet his bees make honey.

[Exit Fidelio.

CARLOTTA (*looking after him*). 'Tis the one wise fool
We have among us.

[Enter Grazia.

GRAZIA. Oh, here you are, my ducklings!
Always together, like a beggar and a flea!
I looked for you at dinner-time; I forget now
What for; but then 'twas a matter of more weight
Than laying siege to a city, — la, how time
Does carry one on! An hour is like an ocean,
The way it separates you from yourself! —
(*To Bianca and Beatrice*) What do you find to talk
about all day?

BEATRICE. We do not talk all day.

CARLOTTA. Nay, 'tis you, Grazia,
That talk all day.

BEATRICE. We ride, and play at tennis.

BIANCA. 'Tis you that ride, Beatrice. I but mount
On a heaving hill, and strive my best to stick there.

GRAZIA. I' faith, I have seen you going forth, — you
sidewise
Aslant your pretty palfrey; and Her Highness,
As God, my judge, astride the devil himself.

BEATRICE. What, Cupid? — La, he's gentle as a
kitten!
Though he's a little young, 'tis true, not settled yet
In his mind.

LAURA.   As to his mind, 'twere a small matter,
Were he a bit more settled in his legs!

GRAZIA. What did I come here for? — I must go
back
To where I started, and think of it again!
[Exit Grazia.

CARLOTTA (calling after her). Are you sure that you
remember where you started?
— — The woman hath a head like a sieve.

LAURA.   And yet,
You may be sure 'tis nothing more than the thimble
Of the matter she's forgotten. I never knew her
Mislay the thread or the needle of a thing.

BIANCA.   We must study now, Beatrice, we indeed
      must.

We have not opened a book since yesterday.

LAURA.   La, as for me, I have not opened a book
      Since yesteryear. — I'd liefer open a vein!

CARLOTTA.   Lessons, — troth, I remember well those
      lessons.

As for what I learned, — troth, that's a different
      matter.

FRANCESCA.   'Tis curious; the things that one re-
      members

Are foolish things.   One does not know at all
      Why one remembers them.   There was a blackbird
      With a broken foot somebody found and tamed
      And named Euripides! — I can see it now.

CARLOTTA.   Some of the silly rhymes we used to write
      In the margins of our books, I still remember!

LAURA.   And eating sweets behind the covers of them!

FRANCESCA.   And faces — faces — faces — and a little
      game

We used to play, all marching in a row
      And singing! — I wish I were a child again.

BEATRICE.   You are not old, Francesca.   You are very
      young.

And very beautiful!

FRANCESCA.   I have been beautiful
Too many years to be so very young.

CARLOTTA. How now, Francesca! Would you have
it said
You are enamoured of some beardless youth,
That so you see the wrinkles suddenly?
Have done! Have done!

BIANCA.   Where shall we study, Bice?

BEATRICE. Indoors. I cannot study out of doors.
[*Exeunt Beatrice and Bianca.*

LAURA. I vow I never knew a pair of lovers
More constant than those two.

CARLOTTA.   A pair of lovers?
Marry, I find your figure lacking force!
Since when were lovers true?

FRANCESCA.   Oh, peace, Carlotta!
You bear too sharp a weapon against the world, —
A split tongue full of poison, in a head
That darts at every heel! — I'm going in.
[*Exit Francesca.*

LAURA. You should not say such things when she is
with us, Carlotta.

CARLOTTA. Is the woman in love?

LAURA.   In love!

She is so far gone she does not know which way

To sail, — all shores are equally out of sight.

[*Exeunt Laura and Carlotta.*

Music off stage. Enter Fidelio, singing.

FIDELIO.   "What was I doing when the moon stood
        above?

What did I do? What did I do?

I lied to a lady that had given me her love, —

I swore to be true! I swore to be true!"

(*He picks up from the grass a white scarf which
Beatrice was wearing, and which slipped from her
shoulders unnoticed as she went out*)

My mistress!

(*He thrusts the scarf under his cloak and continues
his song, just as Guido enters from another direction*)

"And what was I doing when the sun stood above?

What did I do? What did I do? —"

GUIDO.   By my sacred word, Fidelio,

I do not like your song.

FIDELIO.   Faith, and small wonder! —

It is a song that sets the evil eye

To staring in upon itself.

GUIDO (*stopping in his walk*). What mean you

By that, my throaty friend?

FIDELIO.   I mean to say
That, taking it all in all and by and large,
You have no ear for music.

GUIDO.   I have no ear
For yours, but it is possible Apollo
Had a better tenor. I never heard him sing.

FIDELIO. Nay, and how could you? — He died when
you were born!

GUIDO. He died, that is, in giving birth to me?

FIDELIO. Aye, if you like, — you bear as much resem-
blance
To him as to your mother's husband, surely.

GUIDO. Take care, Fidelio.

FIDELIO (*lightly*).   So! Then it angers you
Apollo should be deemed your sire! I told you
(*sadly*)
You have no ear for music!

GUIDO.   You are a sly fool,
My merry friend. What hide you under the cloak?

FIDELIO. Why, 'tis a little patch of snow the sun
Would lay too hot a hand on.

GUIDO.   By my life, —
And what are you that you can keep the sun

From shining where it will?

FIDELIO.   Why, by your life, —

And a foul oath it is! — why, by your life,

I am a cloud, — that is an easy riddle.

SCENE 2

*A garden with a fountain, at Fiori. Beatrice and
Bianca sitting side by side on a low step. Evening.*

BEATRICE. How beautiful it is to sit like this,

Snow-White, — to think of much, and to say little.

BIANCA. Ay, it is beautiful. I shall remember

All my life long these evenings that we spent

Sitting just here, thinking together. (*Pause*) Rose-
Red,

It is four years to-day since first we met.

Did you know that?

BEATRICE.   Nay, is it?

BIANCA.   Four years to-day.

I liked you from the moment that I saw you,

Beatrice!

BEATRICE. I you, Bianca. From the very moment!

I thought you were the prettiest little girl

That I had ever seen.

BIANCA. I was afraid
Of you, a little, at first, — you were a Princess,
You see. But you explained that being a Princess
Was much the same as anything else. 'Twas nice,
You said, when people were nice, and when they
    were not nice
'Twas hateful, just the same as everything else.
And then I saw your dolls, and they had noses
All scratched, and wigs all matted, just like mine,
Which reassured me even more! — I still, though,
Think of you as a Princess; the way you do things
Is much more wonderful than the way I do them! —
The way you speak to the servants, even the way
You pick up something that you drop.

BEATRICE. You goose!
'Tis not because I'm a Princess you feel that way —
I've always thought the same thing about you! —
The way you draw your gloves on is to me
More marvelous than the way the sun comes up!
(*They both burst out laughing*)
Oh, lud, — how droll we are!

BIANCA. Oh, I shall die
Of laughing! Think you any one else, Rose-Red,
Was ever half so silly?

BEATRICE.   I dare wager
   There be a thousand, in this realm alone,
   Some even sillier!

BIANCA.   Here comes Fidelio!

   [*Enter Fidelio.*

BEATRICE.   Fidelio, sing to us, — there is no nightin-
      gale
   Abroad to-night, save you.   And the night cries
   For music!

BIANCA.   Sing, Fidelio!

FIDELIO.   I have no thorn
   To lean my breast on.   I've been happy all day,
   And happiness ever made a crow of me.

BEATRICE.   Sing, none the less, — unless you have a
      cold,
   Which is a singer's only rock of refuge.
   You have no cold, or you would not be happy.
   So sing.

FIDELIO (*singing*).   "Oh, little rose-tree, bloom!
         Summer is nearly over.
      The dahlias bleed and the phlox is seed,
         Nothing's left of the clover,
      And the path of the poppy no one knows, —
      I would blossom if I were a rose!

Summer for all your guile
  Will brown in a week to autumn,
And launched leaves throw a shadow below
  Over the brook's clear bottom,
And the chariest bud the year can boast
Be brought to bloom by the chastening frost!
Oh, little rose-tree, bloom!"

[*As he finishes the song Fidelio goes out, softly
strumming the last chords. Bianca and Beatrice sit
quite still for a moment.*

BIANCA. Do you know what I am thinking, Bice?

BEATRICE. You're wondering where we'll be ten years
    from now,
  Or something of that nature.

BIANCA.   Ay, I was wondering
  Which would be married first, and go away,
  And would we still be friends.

BEATRICE.   Oh, do you doubt it,
  Snow-White?

BIANCA.   Nay, nay, — I doubt it not, my dear, —
  But I was wondering. I am suddenly sad,
  I know not why. I do not wish to leave you
  Ever.

BEATRICE. I know. I cannot bear to think

Of parting.   We have been happy these four years
Together, have we not?

BIANCA.   Oh, Beatrice!

[*She weeps.*

BEATRICE.   Nay, do not weep! — Come, you must go
to bed.

You are tired to-night. We rode too far to-day.
(*She draws Bianca's head down to her shoulder*)
Oh, you are tired, tired, you are very tired.
You must be rocked to sleep, and tucked in bed,
And have your eyelids kissed to make you dream
Of fairies!   Come, dear, come.

BIANCA.   Oh, I do love you,
Rose-Red!   You are so sweet!   Oh, I do love you
So much! — so much!   I never loved anyone
The way that I love you!   There is nobody
In all the world so wonderful as you!

[*She throws her arms about Beatrice and clings to
her.*

SCENE 3

*A room in the palace at Fiori.   Lorenzo and Beatrice
playing chess.   Twilight.*

LORENZO. You'll not be able to get out of that,

I think, my girl, with both your castles gone.

BEATRICE. Be not so sure! — I have a horse still,
father,

And in a strong position: if I move him here,

You lose your bishop; and if you take my bishop,

You lose your queen.

LORENZO.   True, but with my two rooks

Set here, where I can push them back and forth,

My king is safe till worms come in to eat him.

BEATRICE. What say you then to this? — Will you
take this pawn,

Or will you not?

LORENZO (*studying the board*). Od's bones! — where
did that come from?

[*Enter Octavia.*

OCTAVIA. La, would you lose your eyesight, both of
you? —

Fumbling about those chessmen in the dark?

You, Beatrice, at least, should have more wit!

LORENZO. "At least" — hm! — Did you hear her
say, "at least,"

Bice, my daughter?

BEATRICE.   Ay. But it is true

The twilight comes before one knows it.

LORENZO.   Ay,

'Tis true, but unimportant. Nevertheless,
I am a tractable old fellow. — Look you,
I will but stay to map the lay of the pieces
Upon this bit of letter. 'Tis from a king
Who could not tell the bishop from the board, —
And yet went blind at forty. — A little chess
By twilight, mark you, and all might have been well.
[*Enter Bianca.*

BIANCA. Oh, — I've been looking everywhere for you?

OCTAVIA (*drily*). For me?

BIANCA.   Nay, mother, — for Beatrice. Bice,
The rose is out at last upon that bush
That never blossomed before, — and it is white
As linen, just as I said 'twould be!

BEATRICE.   Why, the bud
Was redder than a radish!

BIANCA.   Ay, I know.
But the blossom's white, pure white. Come out and
see!
(*Politely*) Would you like to see it, mother?

OCTAVIA.   Nay, not now, child.
Some other time.

BEATRICE.   Father, we'll end the game
  To-morrow; and do you not be scheming at it
  All night!

LORENZO.   Nay, I will not unfold the chart.

BEATRICE. But you remember well enough without;
  Promise me not to think of it.

LORENZO.   I' faith,
  You are a desperate woman. Ay, I promise.
  [*Exeunt Bianca and Beatrice. Octavia seats herself.
  Pause.*

OCTAVIA. I tell you, as I've told you often before,
  Lorenzo, 'tis not good for two young girls
  To be so much together!

LORENZO.   As you say.

OCTAVIA. For myself, I must confess
  It seems a natural thing, enough, that youth
  Should seek out youth. And if they are better
    pleased
  Talking together than listening to us,
  I find it not unnatural. What have we
  To say to children? — They are as different
  From older folk as fairies are from them.

OCTAVIA. "Talking together," Lorenzo! What have
    they

To talk about, save things they might much better
Leave undiscussed? — you know what I mean, —
    lovers,
And marriage, and all that — if that be all!
One never knows — it is impossible
To hear what they are saying; they either speak
In whispers, or burst out in fits of laughter
At some incredible nonsense. There is nothing
So silly as young girls at just that age. —
At just Bianca's age, that is to say.
As for the other, — as for Beatrice,
She's older than Bianca, and I'll not have her
Putting ideas into my daughter's head!

LORENZO. Fear not, my love. Your daughter's head
    will doubtless,
In its good time, put up its pretty hair,
Chatter, fall dumb, go moping in the rain,
Be turned by flattery, be bowed with weeping,
Grow gray, and shake with palsy over a staff, —
All this, my love, as empty of ideas
As even the fondest mother's heart could wish.

OCTAVIA. You mock me, sir?

LORENZO.   I am but musing aloud,
As is my fashion. — And indeed, my dear,

What is the harm in lovers-and-all-that
That virtuous maidens may not pass the time
With pretty tales about them? — After all,
Were it not for the years of looking forward to it
And looking back upon it, love would be
Only the commonest bird-song in the hedge, —
And men would have more time to think, —and less
To think about.

OCTAVIA.   That may be. But young girls
Should not be left alone too much together.
They grow too much attached. They grow to feel
They cannot breathe apart. It is unhealthy.

LORENZO. It may be true. But as for me, whom youth
Abandoned long ago, I look on youth
As something fresh and sweet, like a young green tree,
Though the wind bend it double. — 'Tis you, 'tis I,
'Tis middle age the fungus settles on.

OCTAVIA. Your head is full of images. You have
No answers. I shall do as I spoke of doing,
And separate them for a little while,
Six months, maybe a year. I shall send Bianca

Away within a fortnight. That will cure them.
I know. I know. Such friendships do not last.

CURTAIN

ACT II

SCENE 1 — *Four months later*

*A garden, near the palace at Fiori. The young Duke
Guido is discovered standing with one foot resting on
a garden bench, looking off, lost in thought. Enter
Giovanni.*

GIOVANNI. That is a merry face you wear, my Guido!
Now that the young King Mario visits the court
And walks all morning in the woods with the Prin-
cess,
Or gives her fencing lessons, — upon my word,
You are as gay as a gallows!

GUIDO.   She is never
Alone with him. Laura — Carlotta — some one
Is always there.

GIOVANNI.   Ah — ah — but even so,
No matter who is there, I tell you, lovers
Are always alone!

GUIDO. Why do you say these things,
Giovanni?

GIOVANNI. Because I love you, you lean wolf,
And love to watch you snuff the air. My friend,
There was a time I thought it all ambition
With you, a secret itching to be king —
And not so secret, either — an open plot
To marry a girl who will be Queen some morning.
But now at times I wonder. You have a look
As of a man that's nightly gnawed by rats,
The very visage of a man in love.
Is it not so?

GUIDO. I do not know, Giovanni.
I know I have a passion in my stomach
So bitter I can taste it on my tongue.
She hates me. And her hatred draws me to her
As the moon draws the tide.

GIOVANNI. You are like a cat —
There never was a woman yet that feared you
And shunned you, but you leapt upon her shoulder!
Well, I'll be off. The prettiest girl in Fiori, —
Unless it be Her Highness, waits for me
By a fountain. All day long she sells blue plums,
And in the evening what she has left of them

She gives to me! You should love simply, Guido,
As I do.

[*Exit Giovanni.*

Guido sits on the bench and drops his head in his
hand. Enter Francesca.

FRANCESCA (*softly*). Guido! Guido!

GUIDO.   Who calls me?

FRANCESCA. Guido!

GUIDO. Francesca! Why do you follow me here? —
    You know I do not wish to see you!

FRANCESCA.   Do not be angry.
  'Tis half a week since you have spoken to me,
  And more than a week since you have so much as
      laid
  Your hand upon my arm! And do you think,
  Loving you as I do, I can do without you,
  Forever, Guido, and make no sign at all?
  I know you said you did not wish to see me
  Ever again, — but it was only a quarrel —
  And we have quarreled before!

GUIDO.   It was not a quarrel.
  I am tired of you, Francesca. You are too soft.
  You weep too much.

FRANCESCA.   I do not weep the less

For having known you.

GUIDO.   So; — it will save you tears, then,
To know me less.

FRANCESCA.   Oh, Guido, how your face
Is changed, — I cannot think those are the eyes
That looked into my eyes a month ago!
What's come between us?

GUIDO.   Nothing has come between us.
It is the simple snapping of a string
Too often played upon.

FRANCESCA.   Ah! — but I know
Who snapped it! It will do you little good
To look at her, — she'll never look at you!

GUIDO.   Be silent a moment! — Unless you would be
Silent longer!

FRANCESCA.   Indeed! I shall speak out my mind!
You go beyond yourself! There is proportion
Even in nature like my own, that's twisted
From too much clinging to a crooked tree!
And this is sure: if you no longer love me,
You shall no longer strike me!

MARIO (off stage).   Beatrice!
Wait for me! Wait!

BEATRICE (off stage). Not I! Who does not run

As fast as I run, shall be left behind me!

GUIDO. They are coming here! I do not wish to see
them!

FRANCESCA. Oh, Guido!

[*She follows him off. Exeunt Guido and Francesca.*
Enter Beatrice, running, followed by Mario.

MARIO.   Beatrice, you run like a boy!
You whistle like a boy! And upon my word,
You are the only girl I ever played
At jousting with, that did not hold her sword
As if it were a needle! Which of us,
Think you, when we are married, will be King?

BEATRICE. When we are married! Sir, I'll have you
know
There's an ogre to be tamed, a gem to be pried
From out a dragon's forehead, and three riddles
To be solved, each tighter than the last, before
A Princess may be wed!

MARIO.   Even by a King?

BEATRICE. For Kings the rules are sterner!— One
more riddle,
And a mirror that will show her always young.

MARIO. And if I do these things, then, will you have
me, Rose-Red?

BEATRICE. Maybe. And if you do not do them,
Maybe. Come — I will race you to the bridge!

MARIO (*catching her hand*). Nay, not so fast! —
Have you no wish to be
Beside me, ever, that you are forever running
Ahead?

BEATRICE. Indeed, if you would have the truth
It has come into my mind more times than once
It would be sweet to be beside you often.

MARIO. Rose-Red!

BEATRICE. Come — I will race you to the bridge!

[*Exeunt Beatrice and Mario.*

SCENE 2

Courtyard of the palace at Fiori. Entire court assembled. A band of strolling players, with a little stage on wheels, are doing a Harlequinade pantomime to amuse the young King Mario, the guest of honor. Beatrice sits beside him. In this scene the two people who are oblivious to the pantomime are Guido and Octavia. Guido is apparently brooding over something. From time to time he looks at Beatrice and Mario.

Once, having gazed for some moments at the pair,

he looks at Octavia and sees that she, too, is looking at them, which seems to satisfy him. The Queen does not take her eyes from the two during the entire scene. Beatrice and Mario do not conduct themselves precisely as lovers, but they are very gay and happy to be in each other's company, apparently. Lorenzo watches the show with a benign, almost childish interest. Pantomime begins.

GIOVANNI. You, Pierrot, are you not a little thick
    For such a sorrowful fellow?

PIERROT.   Nay, indeed!
    Sorrow may come to all. And 'tis amazing
    How much a man may live through and keep fat.
    [Pantomime continues.

CARLOTTA. Ho! Now he stumbles! Look you, Pantaloon,
    If you were not so learned i' the head
    You might know better where to put your feet!

LAURA (*to Carlotta*). 'Tis curious how it addles a man's bones
    To think too much.

CARLOTTA.   Nay, truth. Wise men were ever
    Awkward i' the legs.
    [Pantomime continues.

RAFFAELE.   Have at him, Polichinello.

GIOVANNI. Lay on! Lay on!

ANSELMO.   Leave not a nail of him!

GIOVANNI. Dog! Would you have him write a book
about you?

LUIGI. Spit him i' the liver! It is his only organ!

BEATRICE (*to Mario*). Nay, it is cruel. I cannot look
at it.

MARIO. It is but play.

BEATRICE.   Ay, but 'tis cruel play.
To be so mocked at! — Come, take heart, good
Doctor!
'Tis a noisy fellow, but light withal! — Blow at
him!

GIOVANNI (*to Guido*). She has the softest heart that
ever I saw
In a hard woman. It may be, seeing she has pity
For one rogue, she has pity for another!
Mark you, my Guido, there is hope yet!

GUIDO.   Nay,
There's not. I have opened up my mind to her,
And she will none of me.

GIOVANNI (*jestingly*).   That was the last thing

You should have done! — Speak, — did she give for
    answer

She loves the King?

GUIDO.   Not she. She gave for answer
She does not love the Duke.

[*Pantomime continues.*

ANSELMO (*to Colombine*).   Ah, pretty lady!

CARLOTTA. La, she is fickle! How she turns from one
    face

To another face, — and smiles into them all!

FRANCESCA. Oh, ay, but 'tis the Pierrot that she loves.

[*Pantomime continues and comes to a close. All ap-
plaud.*

LUIGI. Well done!

ANSELMO.   Bravo!

GIOVANNI.   A monstrous lively play!

BEATRICE. Oh, is it over? — I would it were not over!

MARIO. And yet it pleased you not!

BEATRICE.   When it pleased me not,
I looked at you.

MARIO.   And when I pleased you not — ?

BEATRICE. I looked at Harlequin. However, I saw
    him

But fleetingly. Pray, was he dark or fair?

LUIGI. Laura!

LAURA. Who calls? La, it is only Luigi!

LUIGI. Laura, there'll be a moon to-night.

LAURA. I' faith,
There was a moon last night.
[*She sighs.*

LUIGI. At ten o'clock,
Were I by a certain gate, would you be there?
What say you?

LAURA. Ay, — if weariness overtook me,
And I could not get further!

CARLOTTA. La, 'tis sundown!
[*In the meantime the crowd has been breaking up
and dispersing. The curtain falls on the disappearing
spectators and on Pierrot and his troupe packing up
their wagon to go to the next town.*

SCENE 3

*Fiori. A garden with a fountain. Evening. Enter
Octavia and ladies.*

OCTAVIA. It would amuse me if I had a lily
To carry in my hand. You there, Carlotta!
You have a long arm, — plunge it in the pool

And fish me forth a lily!

CLAUDIA.   Majesty,

They close at night.

OCTAVIA.   Well — we will open them.

CARLOTTA (*going to pool and scanning it*). Go to —
I am not a frog!

OCTAVIA. What did you say?

ARIANNA. She says she sees a frog, Your Majesty.

FRANCESCA (*aside to Carlotta*). You are mad! Can
you not keep your tongue in your head?

CARLOTTA. Ay, I can keep it in my cheek. — There's
one.

God grant it have an eel at the end of it, —
I'll give the dame good measure.

[*While the ladies are at the pool, enter Guido.*

GUIDO.   Greeting, madam!

OCTAVIA. Who greets me? — Ah, it is the Duke.
Good even,

Guido. You seek an audience with me?

GUIDO. Nay — nay — but if you send away your
women, —

We shall be more alone.

OCTAVIA (*after considering him a moment*). You may
leave me now,

Laura, Francesca — all of you — and you would
   best go in
At an early hour, instead of walking the gardens
All night; I would have you with your wits
About you in the morning.

CARLOTTA (*aside*).   Oh, indeed?
You would best go in yourself, lest the dew rust you,
You sauce-pan!
[*Exeunt ladies.*

OCTAVIA. Now, my good sir, — you may speak.

GUIDO (*as if by way of conversation*). It is a long
   time, is it not, your daughter —
Is absent from the court?

OCTAVIA.   Why say you that?

GUIDO. Why but to pass the time, till she returns?

OCTAVIA. Nay, Guido. That is well enough for
   some,
But not for me. I know the slant of your fancy;
'Tis not in that direction.

GUIDO.   Yet methinks
The sooner she is back again at court
The happier for us both.

OCTAVIA.   "Us both"? What "both"?

GUIDO. You, madam, and myself.

OCTAVIA.   And why for me?

GUIDO (*carefully*). Why, are you not her mother?

OCTAVIA.   Hah! (*Pause*) Guido,
What festers in your mind? Do you speak out now,
If you await some aid from me.

GUIDO.   Madam,
I have but this to say: if I were a woman
With a marriageable daughter, and a King rode by,
I'd have her at the window.

OCTAVIA.   So. I thought so.
(*With an entire change of manner*)
Guido, what think you, — does she love the King, —
I mean Lorenzo's daughter?

GUIDO.   Ah, she loves him.

OCTAVIA. And loves he her?

GUIDO.   Oh, ay. He loves the moon,
The wind in the cypress trees, his mother's portrait
At seventeen, himself, his future children —
He loves her well enough. But had she blue eyes
And yellow hair, and were afraid of snakes,
He yet might love her more.

OCTAVIA.   You think so, Guido?
I am content to learn you of that mind.
There had occurred to me — some time ago,

In fact — a similar fancy. And already
My daughter is well on her way home.
[*Exeunt Guido and Octavia.*
*Music. Enter Beatrice and Fidelio. Fidelio strums
his lute softly throughout the next conversation, up
to the words, "and cease to mock me."*

BEATRICE. Fidelio,
Were you ever in love?

FIDELIO. I was never out of it.

BEATRICE. But truly?

FIDELIO. Well, I was only out of it
What time it takes a man to right himself
And once again lose balance. Ah, indeed,
'Tis good to be in love. I have often noticed,
The moment I fall out of love, that moment
I catch a cold.

BEATRICE. Are you in love, then, now?

FIDELIO. Ay, to be sure.

BEATRICE. Oh! Oh! With whom, Fidelio?
Tell me with whom!

FIDELIO. Why, marry, with yourself, —
That are the nearest to me, — and by the same
troth,
The farthest away.

BEATRICE. Go to, Fidelio!
I am in earnest, and you trifle with me
As if I were a child.

FIDELIO. Are you not a child, then?

BEATRICE. Not any more.

FIDELIO. How so?

BEATRICE. I am in love.

FIDELIO. Oh — oh — oh, misery, misery, misery,
misery!

BEATRICE. Why do you say that?

FIDELIO. Say what?

BEATRICE. "Misery, misery."

FIDELIO. It is a song.

BEATRICE. A song?

FIDELIO. Ay, 'tis a love-song.
Oh, misery, misery, misery, misery, oh!

BEATRICE. Nay, sweet Fidelio, be not so unkind!
I tell you, for the first time in my life
I am in love! Do you be mannerly now,
And cease to mock me.

FIDELIO. What would you have me do?

BEATRICE. I would have you shake your head, and pat
my shoulder,
And smile and say, "Godspeed."

FIDELIO (*doing so very tenderly*).   Godspeed.

BEATRICE (*bursting into tears*).   I' faith
I do not know if I am happy or sad.
But I am greatly moved.   I would Bianca
Were here.   I never lacked her near so much
As to-night I do, although I lack her always.
She is a long time gone. — If I tell you something,
Will you promise not to tell?

FIDELIO.   Nay, I'll not promise,
But I'll not tell.

BEATRICE.   Fidelio, I do love so
The King from Lagoverde!   I do so love him!

FIDELIO.   Godspeed, Godspeed.

BEATRICE.   Ay, it is passing strange:
Last week I was a child, but now I am not.
And I begin my womanhood with weeping;
I know not why. — La, what a fool I am!
'Tis over.   Sing, Fidelio.

FIDELIO.   Would you a gay song,
My Princess?

BEATRICE.   Ay. — And yet — nay, not so gay.
A simple song, such as a country-boy
Might sing his country-sweetheart. — Is it the moon
Hath struck me, do you think?   I swear by the moon

I am most melancholy soft, and most
Outrageous sentimental! Sing, dear fool.
FIDELIO (*singing*).

> "Butterflies are white and blue
> In this field we wander through.
> Suffer me to take your hand.
> Death comes in a day or two.
> All the things we ever knew
> Will be ashes in that hour.
> Mark the transient butterfly,
> How he hangs upon the flower.
> Suffer me to take your hand.
> Suffer me to cherish you
> Till the dawn is in the sky.
> Whether I be false or true,
> Death comes in a day or two."

CURTAIN

ACT III

SCENE I. *The following summer*

A field or meadow near Fiori. As the curtain rises voices are heard off stage singing a bridal song.

Song: "Strew we flowers on their pathway!
        Bride and bridegroom, go you sweetly.
        There are roses on your pathway.
        Bride and bridegroom, go you sweetly.
        Sweetly live together."

*Enter Viola, Lilina, Lela, Arianna, and Claudia,
laden with garlands, flowering boughs and baskets of
flowers. They meet Anselmo coming from another
direction, also bearing flowers.*

VIOLA. How beautiful, Anselmo! Where did you find
    them?

ANSELMO. Close by the brook.

LILINA.   You gathered all there were?

ANSELMO. Not by one hundredth part.

LELA.   Nay, is it true?

We must have more of them!

ARIANNA.   And are they fragrant

As well?

ANSELMO. Ay, by my heart, they are so sweet

I near to fainted climbing the bank with them.

*[The ladies cluster about Anselmo and smell the
flowers.*

LILINA. Oh!

VIOLA.   Ah!

CLAUDIA. How drowsily sweet!

LELA. Oh, sweet!

ARIANNA. What fragrance!

[*Enter Laura and Giovanni, followed by Carlotta and· Raffaele.*

LAURA. La, by my lung! I am as out of breath
As a babe new-born! Whew! Let me catch the air!

[*She drops her flowers and seats herself beside them.*

CARLOTTA (*to the younger ladies and Anselmo, by way of greeting*). How hot the sun is getting!

ANSELMO. 'Tis nigh noon,
I think.

GIOVANNI. 'Tis noon.

CLAUDIA. We must be starting back.

LAURA. Not till I get my breath.

RAFFAELE. Come, — I will
fan you.

[*He fans her with a branch.*

LAURA. 'Tis good — 'tis very good — oh, peace — oh,
slumber —
Oh, all good things! You are a proper youth.
You are a zephyr. I would have you fan me
Till you fall dead.

CARLOTTA. I tell you when it comes

To gathering flowers, much is to be said
For spreading sheets on the grass, — it gives you less
The backache.

LAURA.   Nobly uttered, my sweet bird.

GIOVANNI. Yet brides must have bouquets.

CARLOTTA.   And sit at home,
Nursing complexions, whilst I gather them.

LILINA (*running to Carlotta, along with Lela and
Viola, and throwing her arms about her*).
Nay, out upon you now; Carlotta! Cease now
To grumble so, — 'tis such a pretty day!

VIOLA. And weddings mean a ball!

                         And one may dance all night
At weddings!

LILINA.   Till one needs must dance to bed,
Because one cannot walk there!

GIOVANNI.   And one eats
Such excellent food!

ANSELMO.   And drinks such excellent wine!

CLAUDIA. And seldom will you see a bride and
Bridegroom more beautiful and gracious, or whom
Garlands do more become.

GIOVANNI.   'Tis so, — upon my sword! —

Which I neglected to bring with me — 'tis so,
Upon Anselmo's sword!

CARLOTTA.   Nay, look you, Laura!
You must not fall asleep! (*To Raffaele*) Have
   done, you devil!
Is it a poppy that you have there? (*To Laura*)
Look you, we must be starting back!

[*Laura rouses, then falls back again.*

LAURA.   Ay, that we must.

ARIANNA. Where are the others?

ANSELMO.   Scattered all about.
I will call to them. Hola! You fauns and dryads!
Where are you?

VOICES.   Here! Here! Is it time to go?

ANSELMO. Come this way! We are starting back!

VOICES.   We are coming!
We'll come in a moment! I cannot bear to leave
This place!

GIOVANNI (*as they enter*). A thousand greetings, lovely
   Clara!
Lucia, a thousand greetings! How now, Luigi!
I know you, man, despite this soft disguise!
You are no flower-girl!

LUIGI.   I am a draught-horse,

That's what I am, for four unyielding women!
Were I a flower-girl, I'd sell the lot
For a bit of bread and meat — I am so hungry
I could eat a butterfly!

CARLOTTA.　　　　　　What ho, Francesca!
I have not seen you since the sun came up!

FRANCESCA.　This is not I, — I shall not be myself
Till it goes down!

LELA.　　　　　　Oh, la, what lovely lilies!

FRANCESCA.　Be tender with them — I risked my life
to get them!

LILINA.　Where were they?

FRANCESCA.　　　　　Troth, I do not know.
I think they were in a dragon's mouth.

LAURA (*suddenly waking*).　　Well, are we going?
[*All laugh.*

LUIGI.　No one is going that cannot go afoot.
I have enough to carry!

LAURA.　　　　　　Nay, take me too!
I am a little thing. What does it matter —
One flower more?

LUIGI.　　　　　You are a thousand flowers,
Sweet Laura, — you are a meadow full of them —
I'll bring a wagon for you.

CARLOTTA.   Come.   Come home.

[*In the meantime the stage has been filling with girls
and men bearing flowers, a multitude of people, in
groups and couples, humming the song very softly.
As Carlotta speaks several more people take up the
song, then finally the whole crowd.   They move off
slowly, singing.*

SONG: "Strew we flowers on their pathway," etc.

SCENE 2

*Bianca's boudoir in the palace at Fiori.   Bianca, with
a mirror in her hand, having her hair done by a maid.
Several maids about, holding perfume flasks, brushes,
and veils, articles of apparel of one sort or another.
Beatrice standing beside her, watching.*

BIANCA.   Look at me, Rose-Red. Am I pretty enough,
    Think you, to marry a King?

BEATRICE.   You are too pretty.
    There is no justice in it.   Marry a cobbler
    And make a king of him.   It is unequal, —
    Here is one beggarly boy king in his own right,
    And king by right of you.

BIANCA.   Mario is not

A beggarly boy! Nay, tell me truly, Bice,
What do you think of him?

BEATRICE. La, by my soul!
Have I not told you what I think of him
A thousand times? He is graceful enough, I tell you,
And hath a well-shaped head.

BIANCA. Nay, is that all?

BEATRICE. Nay, hands and feet he hath, like any
other.

BIANCA. Oh, out upon you for a surly baggage!
Why will you tease me so? You do not like him,
I think.

BEATRICE. Snow-White! 'Forgive me! La, indeed,
I was but jesting! By my sacred word,
These brides are serious folk.

BIANCA. I could not bear
To wed a man that was displeasing to you.
Loving him as I do, I could not choose
But wed him, if he wished it, but 'twould hurt me
To think he did not please you.

BEATRICE. Let me, then,
Set your sweet heart at rest. You could not find
In Christendom a man would please me more.

BIANCA. Then I am happy.

BEATRICE.   Ay, be happy, child.

BIANCA.   Why do you call me child?

BEATRICE.   Faith, 'tis the
Season o' the year when I am older than you.
Besides, a bride is always younger than a spinster.

BIANCA.   A spinster! Do you come here to me,
Rose-Red, whilst I pinch you smartly! You,
Arianna, push me Her Highness over here,
That I may pinch her!
(*To Loretta*) Nay, is it finished? Ay, 'tis very well.
Though not so well, Loretta, as many a day
When I was doing nothing! — Nay, my girl,
'Tis well enough.   He will take me as I am
Or leave me as I was.   You may come back
In half an hour, if you are grieved about it,
And do it again.   But go now, — all of you.
I wish to be alone.   (*To Beatrice*)   Not you.
[*Exeunt all but Beatrice and Bianca.*

                              Oh, Rose-Red,
I trust 'twill not be long before I see you
As happy as you see me now!

BEATRICE.   Indeed,
I could not well be happier than I am.
You do not know, maybe, how much I love you.

BIANCA.   Ah, but I do, — I have a measure for it!

BEATRICE.   Ay, for to-day you have. But not for long.
  They say a bride forgets her friends, —* she cleaves so
  To her new lord.   It cannot but be true.
  You will be gone from me.   There will be much
  To drive me from your mind.

BIANCA.   Shall I forget, then,
  When I am old, I ever was a child?
  I tell you I shall never think of you
  Throughout my life, without such tenderness
  As breaks the heart, — and I shall think of you
  Whenever I am most happy, whenever I am
  Most sad, whenever I see a beautiful thing.
  You are a burning lamp to me, a flame
  The wind cannot blow out, and I shall hold you
  High in my hand against whatever darkness.

BEATRICE.   You are to me a silver bell in a tower.
  And when it rings I know I am near home.

SCENE 3

A room in the palace. Mario alone. Enter Beatrice.

BEATRICE.   Mario! I have a message for you! — Nay,
  You need not hang your head and shun me, Mario,

Because you loved me once a little and now
Love somebody else much more. The going of love
Is no less honest than the coming of it.
It is a human thing.

MARIO.   Oh, Beatrice!
What can I say to you?

BEATRICE.   Nay, but indeed,
Say nothing. All is said. I need no words
To tell me you have been troubled in your heart,
Thinking of me.

MARIO.   What can I say to you!

BEATRICE. I tell you, my dear friend, you must forget
This thing that makes you sad. I have forgotten,
In seeing her so happy, that ever I wished
For happiness myself. Indeed, indeed,
I am much happier in her happiness
Than if it were my own; 'tis doubly dear,
I feel it in myself, yet all the time
I know it to be hers, and am twice glad.

MARIO. I could be on my knees to you a lifetime,
Nor pay you half the homage is your due.

BEATRICE. Pay me no homage, Mario, — but if it be
I have your friendship, I shall treasure it.

MARIO. That you will have always.

BEATRICE.   Then you will promise me
Never to let her know. I never told her
How it was with us, or that I cherished you
More than another. It was on my tongue to tell her
The moment she returned, but she had seen you
Already on the bridge as she went by,
And had leaned out to look at you, it seems,
And you were looking at her, — and the first words
She said, after she kissed me, were, "Oh, sister,
I have looked at last by daylight on the man
I see in my dreams!"

MARIO (*tenderly*).   Did she say that?

BEATRICE (*drily*).   Ay, that
Was what she said. — By which I knew, you see,
My dream was over, — it could not but be you.
So that I said no word, but my quick blood
Went suddenly quiet in my veins, and I felt
Years older than Bianca. I drew her head
Down to my shoulder, that she might not see
    my face,
And she spoke on and on. You must not tell her,
Even when you both are old and there is nothing
To do but to remember. She would be withered
With pity for me. She holds me very dear.

MARIO.   I promise it, Rose-Red.   And oh, believe me,
I said no word to you last year that is not
As true to-day!   I hold you still the noblest
Of women, and the bravest.   I have not changed.
Only last year I did not know I could love
As I love now.   Her gentleness has crept so
Into my heart, it never will be out.
That she should turn to me and cling to me
And let me shelter her, is the great wonder
Of the world.   You stand alone.   You need no
    shelter,
Rose-Red.

BEATRICE.   It may be so.

MARIO.   Will you forgive me?

BEATRICE.   I had not thought of that.   If it will
    please you,
Ay, surely. — And now, the reason for my coming:
I have a message for you, of such vast import
She could not trust it to a liv'ried page,
Or even a courier.   She bids me tell you
She loves you still, although you have been parted
Since four o'clock.

MARIO (*happily*).   Did she say that?

BEATRICE.   Ay, Mario.

I must return to her.   It is not long now
Till she will leave me.

MARIO.   She will never leave you,
She tells me, in her heart.

BEATRICE (*happily*).   Did she say that?

MARIO.   Ay, that she did, and I was jealous of you
One moment, till I called myself a fool.

BEATRICE.   Nay, Mario, she does not take from you
To give to me; and I am most content
She told you that.   I will go now.   Farewell,
Mario!

MARIO.   Nay, we shall meet again, Beatrice!

SCENE 4

*The ballroom of the palace at Fiori, raised place in
back, surmounted by two big chairs, for Lorenzo and
Octavia to sit while the dance goes on.   Dais on one
side, well down stage, in full sight of the audience, for
Mario and Bianca.   As the curtain rises, the stage is
empty except for Fidelio, who sits forlornly on the
bottom steps of the raised place in the back of the
stage, his lute across his knees, his head bowed upon
it.   Sound of laughter and conversation, possibly rat-
tling of dishes, off stage, evidently a feast going on.*

LAURA (*off stage*). Be still, or I will heave a plate
at you!

LUIGI (*off stage*). Nay, gentle Laura, heave not the
wedding crockery

At the wedding guest! Behold me on my knees

To tell the world I love you like a fool!

LAURA. Get up, you oaf! Or here's a platter of
gravy

Will add the motley to your folly!

LUIGI. Hold her,

Some piteous fop, that liketh not to see

Fine linen smeared with goose! Oh, gracious Laura,

I never have seen a child sucking an orange

But I wished an orange, too. This wedding irks me

Because 'tis not mine own. Shall we be married

Tuesday or Wednesday?

LAURA. Are you in earnest, Luigi?

LUIGI. Ay, that I am, if never I was before.

LAURA. La, I am lost! I am a married woman!

Water! — Nay, wine will do! On Wednesday,
then.

I'll have it as far off as possible.

[*Enter from banquet-room Guido, Giovanni, and
Raffaele.*

GIOVANNI. Well met, Fidelio! Give us a song!

FIDELIO. Not I!

GUIDO. Why, what is this? You, that are dripping
with song

Week days, are dry of music for a wedding?

FIDELIO. I have a headache. Go and sit in a tree,
And make your own songs.

RAFFAELE. Nay, Fidelio.

String the sweet strings, man!

GIOVANNI. Strike the pretty strings!

GUIDO. Give us the silver strings!

FIDELIO. Nay then, I will that!
(*He tears the strings off the lute and throws them
in Guido's face*)

Here be the strings, my merry gentlemen!

Do you amuse yourself with tying knots in them
And hanging one another! — I have a headache.

[*He runs off, sobbing.*

RAFFAELE. What ails him, think you?

GIOVANNI. Troth, I have no notion.

[*Enter Nurse.*

GUIDO. What ho, good Grazia! I hear the king my
uncle

Is ill again!

GRAZIA.   Where heard you that, you raven?

GUIDO. Marry, I forget. Is't true?

GRAZIA   It is as false
As that you have forgotten where you heard it.
Were you the heir to his power, which I bless God
You're not! — he'd live to hide the throne from you
Full many a long day yet! — Nay, pretty Guido
Your cousin is not yet Queen, — and when she
    is — Faith,
She weareth a wide petticoat, — there'll be
Scant room for you beside her.

[*Exit Nurse across stage.*

GUIDO (*To his companions*).   None the less
I do believe the king is ill.

RAFFAELE.   Who told you?

GUIDO. His wife. She is much exercised about him.

GIOVANNI. 'Tis like enough. This woman would
    rather lie
Than have her breakfast served to her in bed.

[*Exeunt Guido, Giovanni, and Raffaele.*

*Music. Enter Musicians and take place on stage.
Enter four pages and take places on either side the
door from the banquet hall and on either side the
throne in the back. Enter Lorenzo and Octavia,*

*Lorenzo apparently quite well, and seat themselves
on throne in back. Enter courtiers and ladies, Carlotta with Anselmo, Laura with Luigi, etc., and
stand in little groups about the stage, laughing and
talking together. Enter Beatrice alone, her train
held by two pages in black. Enter twelve little
Cupids, running, and do a short dance in the center
of the room, then rush to the empty dais which is
awaiting Mario and Bianca, and cluster about it.
Enter Bianca and Mario, she in white and silver,
with a deep sky-blue velvet train six yards long, held
up by six silver pages (or Cupids); he in black and
gold, with a purple velvet train of the same length
held by six gold pages (or Cupids). His arm is
about her waist, she is leaning back her head against
him and looking up into his face. They come in
slowly, talking softly together, as utterly oblivious
of the court, the pages, the music, everything, as if
they were a shepherd and a shepherdess walking
through a meadow. They walk slowly across the
stage and seat themselves on the dais. The music
changes, strikes up a gay pavane; the ladies and
courtiers dance. Guido, Giovanni, and Raffaele re-
enter just as the music starts and go up to the ladies;*

*Guido goes to Beatrice, and she dances with him.
In the midst of the dance Lorenzo slips a little sidewise in his chair, his head drops forward on his
chest; he does not move again. Nobody notices for
some time. The dance continues, all who are not
dancing watching the dancers, save Octavia, who
watches with great pride and affection Bianca and
Mario, who in turn are looking at one another.
Octavia turns finally to speak to Lorenzo, stares at
him, touches him, then screams. Music stops in
confusion on a discord, dance breaks up wildly,
everybody rushes to throne.*

Scene 5

*The same room later that evening, entirely empty,
disordered. Musicians' benches overturned, a couple
of instruments left about, garlands trampled on the
floor, a wing of one of the Cupids clinging to the dais
of Bianca and Mario. Enter Beatrice, weeping, goes
to her father's throne and creeps up into it, with her
face towards the back of it and clings there, sobbing
quietly. Enter Bianca and Mario.*

BIANCA (*softly*). Ay. She is here. I thought she
would be here.

There are so many people by his bed
Even now, she cannot be alone with him.

MARIO. Is there no hope?

BIANCA. Nay, there is none. 'Tis
over.

He was a kind old man.

MARIO. Come, let us go,
And leave her to herself.

BIANCA. Nay, Mario.
I must not leave her. She will sit like that
All night, unless I bid her come away,
And put her into bed.

MARIO. Will you come to me
After she sleeps?

BIANCA. Ay. If she sleeps.

MARIO. And if not?

BIANCA. I could not leave her.

MARIO. Bianca, do you love me?

BIANCA. Ay, Mario!

MARIO. Ah, but not as I love you!

BIANCA. You do not think that, Mario; you know
How much I love you. But I could not be happy
Thinking of her awake in the darkness, weeping,
And all alone.

MARIO.   Oh, my sweet love!

BIANCA.   It may be
She will sleep.

MARIO.   I shall be waiting for you.
  [*They embrace.*
  [*Exit Mario. Bianca goes to Beatrice and sits at the
  foot of the throne, putting her head against Beatrice's feet.*

BIANCA.   Sister.
  [*After a moment Beatrice slowly reaches down her
  hand, and Bianca takes it.*

CURTAIN

ACT IV

SCENE 1 — *Five years later*

*A marketplace in Fiori, vegetables, fruits, and flow-
ers exposed for sale in little stalls and wagons, crowd
of townspeople moving about, talking, laughing, buy-
ing. Group of children playing a game in a ring.
Supper time.*

CHILDREN. One, two, three,
  The dough is in the oven!

One, two, three,
The bread is on the board!
One, two, three,
The dough is in the oven!
One, two, three,
The bread is on the board!
One, two, three,
All follow me!

EUGENIA. Good-even, Giovanitta. Those are beautiful onions you have there.

GIOVANITTA.   Ay, it has been a good year
For onions.

EUGENIA. I am taking seven.

GIOVANITTA.   Each year,
You buy another onion!

EUGENIA.   Faith, each year
I have another mouth to thrust it in!
Beautiful carrots, too, you have.

GIOVANITTA.   Ay, carrots
Are well enough. One cannot complain. 'Tis a good year
For carrots.

CLARA.   'Tis a good year for many things.
Prices are low, — but not too low for profit.

GIULIANA.   And there are fewer taxes than there once
  were

On things one cannot live without.

ANNA.   'Tis a good Queen
  We have, it must be granted.

GIOVANITTA.   Ay, and a wise one.

GILDA.   And pretty, too.

GIULIANA.   Ho, ho! When did you see her?

GILDA.   This morning, mother. I was at the edge of
  the wood

With Beppo, when they rode by to the hunt,

Talking together, and laughing.

BEPPO (*calling from across the stage*). And the horses
  With feet like this!

[*Arching his hands and feet to represent a horse
  stepping delicately.*

GILDA.   And glittering in the sunshine

In a thousand places, mother! I wanted to tell you

When we returned, but you had gone to the brook

With the linen. They were so near us we could

Hear them talking.

BEPPO (*coming up*). And hear the horses breathe!

ANNA.   What said they?

GILDA.   Well, one of them said — what was the name?

BEPPO.   Anselmo.

GILDA. Oh, ay. She said, "Anselmo, am I getting
   thinner

   Do you think? If I be not thinner than I was at
      starting,

   I shall descend at once! I like not this;

   It chatters my teeth."

BEPPO.   And then she said —

GILDA.   What said she?

   Oh, ay, — about the boat.

BEPPO.   She said, "Next time

   I shall go fishing instead of hunting. A boat

   Hath a more mannerly gait!"

GILDA.   There was one horse, mother,

   That was all white! There was not one hair upon
      him

   That was not white!

GIULIANA.   And who was riding that horse?

BEPPO. A man. And riding well.

GILDA.   He was dressed in green,

   And had a yellow beard. And there was a lady

   With hair the color of Adelina's, bright

   Like fire. She was dressed in blue, and was most
      beautiful.

BEPPO.   And she was mounted on a dappled mare.

GILDA.   But, oh, it was the Queen that was more
   lovely —

Than any of the rest!

GIOVANITTA.   How did you know, now,
   It was the Queen?

GILDA.   Nay, but you could not help
   But know! She was not laughing like the rest, —
   Just smiling; and I should not have been afraid
   To toss a flower to her from the wood,
   If I had had a flower.

BEPPO.   You knew her, though,
   Because she was in scarlet. All the world knows
   She wears a scarlet mantle!

GILDA.   Nay, if that were all,
   It might have been the Pope!

BEPPO.   I would it had been.
   I never saw the Pope.

GILDA.   You never saw
   The Queen until this morning! — Mother, she rides
   Clothed like a man, almost!

BEPPO.   With sword at side!

GILDA.   And, oh, the sword had a jeweled — what is
   the name of it?

BEPPO. Scabbard, of course!

GILDA.   A jeweled scabbard, mother!
I wish I were a queen.

BEPPO.   Ho, you would make
A proper queen, with that droll nose of yours!

GILDA. I know a boy who likes my nose!

BEPPO.   Ho, ho!
He must be a hunchback!

GIULIANA.   You must not tease her, Beppo.

GILDA. I wish I were queen. If I were a queen,
You would not dare to say my nose is droll.

BEPPO. It would be, all the same.

GIOVANITTA.   You should be content
With what you have, not wish to rise beyond it.
It is a sin to covet.

GIULIANA.   Being a queen,
My bird, is not all riding to the hunt
Of a sunny morning.

ANNA.   Nay, 'tis riding back,
At times, of a rainy night, to such a burden
Of cares as simple folk have little mind of.

GILDA. I'd rather have a queen's cares than my own.

BEPPO. Ho, ho! Your cares! What cares have you?

GILDA.   I have

A brother that will be teasing me all times!

'Tis cares enough for one, I tell you.

ADELINA (*across the stage*).   Beppo!

Come help me fetch the milk!

GILDA.   Oh, Mister Beppo,

Your sweetheart calls you! Run and fetch the milk!

LEONORA (*from a house, coming out*). Come in to
supper, children!

RIGO. Oh, not just yet!

ELEANORA. Father's not home yet!

LEONORA.   You need not wait for him.

LOUISA. May we come out again?

LEONORA (*joining other women*). Ay, for a time.

Till it gets dark.

RIGO (*to Louisa*).   'Tis dark now, almost.

LOUISA.   Hush!

She does not know it.

GIULIANA.   'Tis dark now.

LEONORA.   Ay, I know.

I let them play a little after dark

Sometimes, when the weather's fine. I would not
have them

Afraid of shadows. They think I do not know

Darkness from light.

ELEANORA. There's father now!

RIGO. I see him!

[*Eleanora, Louisa and Rigo run off the stage and along the path.*

LEONORA. He is late home to-day. I cannot think
What may have held him. 'Twill be deep night
already
In the woods.

CESCO (*off stage harshly*). Down! Down! Do you
run back to your mother!
See you not I am in haste? — Hang not upon me!

EUGENIA. La! He is in a temper!

LEONORA. I never knew him
So out of patience with them.

GIULIANA. He is hungry, maybe.

LEONORA. He is often hungry, but I never knew him
So out of patience.
(*The children come running back. To Eleanora*)
Why do you weep, my heart?

LUIGI. Father is some one else to-night.

ELEANORA (*weeping*). He pushed me!

[*Enter Cesco, with game on his shoulder.*

SEVERAL WOMEN. Good-even, Cesco.

CESCO (*to Leonora*). Look you, Leonora,

Have we a bed fit for a queen to lie in?

LEONORA.   Nay, faith! Not we!

GILDA.   She can have my bed, mother.

GIULIANA. Ay, true. There is a bed in my house,
    Cesco.

GIOVANITTA. What will the Queen do here?

GIULIANA.   I would indeed
    She had let us know that she was coming!

CESCO.   The Queen
    Knew not herself. Nor is she coming of herself.
    They are bringing her, — on a litter of crossed
        boughs.

GILDA. She is not *dead?*

CESCO.   Nay. Wounded i' the arm
    A little, and in a swoon. But the young King
    Of Lagoverde is no more!

WOMEN.   How so?

CESCO. I tell you my two eyes have looked this day
    On a sad and useless thing! — A fine lad, young,
    And strong, and beautiful as a lad may be,
    And king of a fair country, thrust from horse
    By a foul blow, and sprawled upon the ground, —
    Legs wide asunder, fist full of brown mud,
    Hair in his eyes, — most pitiful unkingly!

Bring me a mug of wine, good wife!

[*Leonora goes out.*

GIOVANITTA.   You, Gilda!

There is a queen you would not be to-night,

I'll warrant you, — the Queen of Lagoverde,

With her two fatherless babes!

EUGENIA.   Nay, now, good Cesco,

What is this matter?

CESCO.   You'll know it quick enough.

They will be bringing the Queen here ere I have breath

To tell you.   They are coming by the road.

I took the mountain path, and ran.

GIULIANA.   I must hasten

To put fresh sheets on.   (*To Gilda*) Look you, — listen well

If he should talk, and tell me afterwards.

[*Exit.*

EUGENIA.   Here comes Horatio!   The boats are in.

[*Some children rush down to the water-side.*

A good day, husband?

HORATIO.   Ay, a heavy day.

What think you of that? — A big one, eh? — Came in

With a school of little fish, — too greedy that time!
What happens here? — The air is full of breathing!
[*The men come up from the boats with children
clinging to them. Beppo and Adelina return from
another direction with the milk.*

LEONORA (*somewhat proudly*). Cesco will tell you.
CESCO. In a word 'tis this: To-day the Queen of Fiori,
Returning from the hunt, is set upon
By brigands; whereat the King of Lagoverde,
Being hunting in that quarter and hearing cries,
Comes up to give his aid; in rendering which
He gives his life as well, and at this moment,
On other men's legs, goes heavily home to supper.
The Queen of Fiori, wounded, and in a swoon
Only less deep than death itself, comes this way.
CROWD. Ay, here they come!
[*Enter Anselmo.*
ANSELMO.
Make way, make way, good people —
Fall back a little — leave a clear space — give air!
[*Enter Laura and Francesca, Luigi, several gentle-
men, and several attendants, four of them bearing a
litter on which lies Beatrice, in a scarlet cloak, her
hair flowing. Luigi is with Laura, who clings to*

*him. If possible to arrange, several of the party
may lead on their horses and lead them off across
the stage. The litter is set down stage in full sight
of the audience. Beppo comes down stage near it,
as does also, from another direction, Gilda. Giuliana returns.*

Who has a bed that we may lay her on?
She cannot leave this place to-night.

GIULIANA.   This way, sir.

[*The attendants pick up the litter and go off, the
crowd following.*

GILDA (*stealing back*). Hist, Beppo!

BEPPO.   Ay?

GILDA.   Heard you not something fall,
When they picked her up again?

BEPPO.   Ay, that I did.

GILDA. What was it, think you? (*They search*) Nay,
    'twas nearer here.

BEPPO. I have it. — 'Tis her sword!

GILDA.   The Queen's? Ay, — truly.
How beautiful.

BEPPO (*slowly and with awe drawing it from its scabbard*)

Look, — there is blood on it!

SCENE 2

A room in the palace at Lagoverde. Bianca and her two little daughters discovered at the rise of the curtain, she in a big chair, they at her feet.

BIANCA. And so the fairy laid a spell on her:
Henceforth she should be ugly as a toad.
But the good fairy, seeing this was done,
And having in no wise power to alter this,
Made all toads beautiful.

LITTLE ROSE-RED.   They are not beautiful
Now, mother!

LITTLE SNOW-WHITE. That was in another country!—
What country, mother?

[Bianca, lost in thought, does not answer.

LITTLE ROSE-RED.   Where is father, mother? —
I have not seen him in so many days!

BIANCA. Father is gone away.

LITTLE ROSE-RED.   Will he come back?

BIANCA. Nay. He will not come back. But we shall
Go where he is.

LITTLE SNOW-WHITE. Soon?

BIANCA.   God grant it may be soon!
Now — shall we play a game?

[*Enter Octavia.*

OCTAVIA. Bianca.

BIANCA. Ay.

OCTAVIA. It is a folly to remain indoors.
Like this. You should be out in the sunshine.

BIANCA. Nay.
I have no business with the sunshine.

OCTAVIA. Ah,
My daughter, say not so! — The children, then, —
They have much need of it, and they have need
Of you, at the same time. Take them without.

BIANCA. I do not wish to be in the sunshine.

LITTLE SNOW-WHITE. Mother,
Come out of doors!

OCTAVIA. You see, now!

BIANCA. Do you run out, dears,
And play at ball. Mother will join you later.

LITTLE ROSE-RED. Where *is* my ball?

BIANCA. Nay, do you not remember?
We put it in the ear of the stone griffin,
Because he hears too much.

LITTLE ROSE-RED. Ay, so we did!

LITTLE SNOW-WHITE. Come on, Rose-Red!

[*Exeunt children.*

OCTAVIA. It is a curious thing
  This friend of yours you rate so monstrous high
  Has not come nigh you in your sore affliction!

BIANCA. I beg you not to speak of that again,
  Mother. 'Tis the third time to-day you have said
    that,
  Or hinted at it. And I answer always,
  "There is some reason for it," as I should answer
  Though you cried daily till the day of doom,
  "It is a curious thing!" There is some reason,
  There is some good reason why she does not come.

OCTAVIA. Oh, ay, I doubt it not! But there are
  Reasons and reasons!

BIANCA. And what am I to learn from that?

OCTAVIA. 'Tis scarce by reason of too much love for
    you
  She leaves you friendless in your greatest need.

BIANCA. I cannot say. 'Tis one thing or another.
  You have no words can turn me to believe
  She has forgotten me, or loves me less.
  'Tis a big thing, to leave me thus alone, —
  And there is some big reason.

OCTAVIA. Ay. Oh, ay.
  'Tis possible she grieves for Mario's death

No less than you.

BIANCA (*simply*).   Ay, it is possible.
I mind she told me on my marriage-day
She was as happy as I.

OCTAVIA.   'Tis a curious thing,
When he was here she came to see you often,
But now that he is gone comes not at all.

BIANCA (*simply*). Ay, it is curious.
   (*Catching Octavia's expression*)
                              Nay, what evil thing
Is in your mind, gives you that evil smile?

OCTAVIA. Only a little thought.

BIANCA.   A little thought,
I'll warrant you! — You'd have me to believe
She loved my husband?

OCTAVIA.   Ay, I know she loved him.

BIANCA. It is a lie!

OCTAVIA.   How dare you say I lie!

BIANCA. Oh, do not be so proud! Let us speak truth
At length, a little! We are so garnished up
With courtesies, so over-sauced and seasoned,
We cannot taste each other! Why do you tell me
A thing like that? — You have no love for me!

OCTAVIA (*weeping*).   I love you too much — you are
    the only thing
  I do love!
BIANCA.   Nay, it is not love of me
  For my own self.   Else would you do the thing
  Would make me happiest.   You know how I have
    loved her,
  Since we were children.   You could not be to me
  What she was; one forgets too many things.
  You could not know my thought.   I loved you
    dearly,
  But you were hard to love; one never knew
  Whether you would be hot or cold to touch.
  Whilst she and I, — oh, we were two young trees
  So nearly of a height we had the same world
  Ever within our vision! — Yet all these years,
  Even from the time we first went to Fiori,
  You have been bearing me your little tales, —
  "She had done this and that, she was thus and so—,"
  Seeking to stir and poison the clear water
  Of my deep love for her!   And now this thing.
  Which is not true.   But if it had been true,
  It would not be so out of all reason cruel
  As that you should have told me of it now.

Nay, do not weep. All day 'tis one of us
Making the other weep. We are two strange,
Unhappy women. Come, let us be at peace.
(*Pause. Bianca rises suddenly*)
Mother, farewell a little while. I go now
To her, seeing that she does not come to me.
But not to question her, not to demand,
"How comes it: this? What can you say to that?"
Only to sit beside her, as in the old days,
And let her lay her quiet on my heart.

SCENE 3

*The garden at Fiori, same as in Act I, Scene 1.
Discovered seated on a stone bench in the sunshine,
Beatrice, clad in a loose gown, looking very ill. Fi-
delio sings off stage.*

FIDELIO (*singing*).

"Let the little birds sing,
  Let the little lambs play.
  Spring is here, and so 'tis spring, —
  But not in the old way.

"I recall a place
  Where a plum-tree grew, —

There you lifted up your face
And blossoms covered you.

"If the little birds sing,
And the little lambs play,
Spring is here, and so 'tis spring, —
But not in the old way."

BEATRICE. It is a pretty song. There be some things
That even the tortured heart's profoundest anguish
Cannot bring down from their high place. Music
Is one of them.

[*Enter Grazia, carrying a bowl.*

GRAZIA.   Now, will you drink this broth,
Or will you not? I swear upon my shroud —
And 'tis a solemn oath — I never nursed
So vaporous a patient! — Come, my bird!

BEATRICE (*taking the bowl, then setting it down*).
Nay, Nurse, I cannot.

GRAZIA.   Oh, alackaday!
What shall I do with you? Come now, and drink
   me
The pretty broth, my dear!

BEATRICE.   I will drink it later.
'Tis too hot.

GRAZIA.   Ay, and in a moment 'twill be
  Too cold! And you'll not drink it! I could cry.
  [*Exit Grazia. Enter Fidelio.*

BEATRICE. Fidelio, an you love me, do you drink this,
  And quickly, man!

FIDELIO (*with grief*). Oh, my dear mistress!

BEATRICE.   Drink!

FIDELIO (*sadly drinking*). I best would leave a little,
    else she'll know
  'Twas never you.

BEATRICE.   Ay, so you would. I' faith,
  It is a knave's trick, but I cannot touch it.
  Go now, Fidelio, ere she come again.
  [*Exit Fidelio. Enter Bianca.*

BIANCA (*softly*). Rose-Red.
  [*Beatrice looks up and listens, thinking it a dream.*

BIANCA.   Rose-Red, dear sister!

BEATRICE (*bowing her head and weeping*). Oh, my
    heart!

BIANCA (*coming towards her*). Why do you weep?

BEATRICE (*looking up startled and seeing her, jumping to her feet*). Oh, no! Oh, God above!
  Go back! Go back!

BIANCA (*amazed, quietly*). Beatrice, are you mad?

'Tis I, Bianca.

BEATRICE (*more quietly*).   Ay, I know 'tis you.

And you must go away.

BIANCA (*breaking down*).   You are mad, my dear!

BEATRICE.   I would I were.   For madmen have their
moments

Of light into the brain. — Hear me, Bianca,

You must return at once to Lagoverde,

And come to me no more, and think of me

No more.

BIANCA.   Ay. I will go.   But ere I go

Tell me you do not love me. 'Tis apparent

You do not.   I but wish to hear the words.

BEATRICE.   Nay, that I will not say.   It would be well,

To say it, and let it be.   But I'll not say it,

It is not true.

BIANCA.   You love me still?

BEATRICE.   I love you

More than all else on earth.   But I have wronged
you

So hugely that I cannot think of it

And stand here talking with you — I am ill — (*She
staggers*)

You must pardon me — I have been very ill —

BIANCA. Then it is true?

BEATRICE (*with a cry as of relief*). Ay, it is true!
Who told you?

BIANCA. My mother told me. I said it was not true.
But if 'tis true — I pity you, Rose-Red.
I pity him. I pity us all together.

BEATRICE (*feverishly*). Ah, I can see it now! — the
quiet road
In the deep wood's gathering darkness, the reins
loose
On the horses' necks, that nodded, nodded, and we
Speaking from time to time, and glad to think
Of home, — and suddenly out of nowhere, — fury,
And faces, and long swords, and a great noise!
And even as I reached to draw my sword,
The arm that held the scabbard set on fire,
As if the sleeve were burning! — and my horse
Backing into the trees, my hair caught, twisted,
Torn out by the roots! Then from the road behind
A second fury! And I turned, confused,
Outraged with pain, and thrust, — and it was
Mario!

BIANCA (*wildly*). What are you, saying? What
are you saying? What is this

You are telling me? That it was you? Your
  hand — ?

Oh, God have mercy upon me! Let me go!

BEATRICE (*pitifully reaching out her arms towards
  her*).

Snow-White! Snow-White! — farewell!

BIANCA (*without turning*). Oh, God have mercy!
  [*Exit Bianca.*

Beatrice falls unconscious to the floor.

CURTAIN

ACT V

SCENE I

A room in the palace at Fiori. Anselmo and Luigi.

LUIGI Nay, is that true, Anselmo?

ANSELMO.   Ay, 'tis true.

But no one saw save me. I drew her sword
Out of his heart and thrust it in its scabbard,
Where she lay senseless.

LUIGI.   Oh, unhappy Queen!

ANSELMO. Ay, she does not forget. Has it not struck
  you

She rides no more? Her black horse stands in stable,
Eating his head off. It is two years now
Since she has visited Lagoverde; and the Queen
Of Lagoverde comes not nigh this place.

LUIGI. There's not the reason that there was to come
Before Octavia's death.

ANSELMO.   Nay, 'tis not that.

LUIGI. Think you that Beatrice told her?

ANSELMO.   Ay,
I doubt it not.

LUIGI.   'Tis hard. They were close friends.

ANSELMO. And since that day her hand upon the
    sceptre
Trembles, — and Guido sees. She goes too much
Among the people, nursing them. She loves them;
Their griefs are hers, their hearts are hers, as well.
But Guido has a following in this court
That hangs upon his word, and he has taught them
Her gentleness is weakness, and her love
Faint-hearted womanish whims, till they are eager
To pull her down, and see a man in place of her.

LUIGI. Her throne is like a raft upon a sea,
That shifts, and rights itself, and may go down
At any moment.

ANSELMO.   The more especially

For all these drowning beggars that cling to it,

Chattering for help.   She will not strike them off.

LUIGI.   Unhappy Queen.   And there's a storm approaching,

If ever I smelled wind.

ANSELMO.   .I fear it, Luigi.

[*Exeunt Anselmo and Luigi.   Enter Guido and
Francesca.*

FRANCESCA.   How do I know you love her still? — I
know,

The way you fall a-tapping with your fingers,

Or plucking at your eyebrows, if her name

Be spoken, or she move across the court.

How do I know? — Oh, Guido, have I learned you

So little, then, in all these bitter years?

I know you very well.

GUIDO.   You know too much!

I'll have an end of this, I tell you!

FRANCESCA.   ·   Ay,

You'd told me that before. — An end of what?

What is this thing you'll put this mighty end to?

'Fore God I would I knew.   Could I but name it,

I might have power to end it then, myself!

GUIDO. I'll have an end of these soft words at twi-
     light,

   And these bad mornings full of bile! I'll have an
     end

   Of all this spying on me!

FRANCESCA (*gently*).   'Tis not so.

   I do not spy upon you. But I see you

   Bigger than other men, and your least gesture —

   A giant moving rocks. — Oh, Guido, tell me

   You do not love her! Even though I know

   You lie, I will believe you, — for I must!

GUIDO (*pause*). Nay, I am done with you. I will
     tell you nothing.

   Out of my way! — I have that on my mind

   Would crush your silly skull like the shell of an
     egg!

   Od's body, will you keep your ugly claws

   From scratching at my sleeve?

   [*He thrusts her roughly aside and rushes out.*

FRANCESCA (*creeping away, sobbing*). Oh, God —
     oh, God —

   I would whatever it is, that it were over.

   [*Exit. Enter Fidelio, and crosses the stage, singing.*

FIDELIO (*singing*).

> "Rain comes down
>
> And hushes the town.
>
> > *And where is the voice that I heard crying?*
>
> Snow settles
>
> Over the nettles.
>
> > *Where is the voice that I heard crying?*
>
> Sand at last
>
> On the drifting mast.
>
> > *And where is the voice .hat I heard crying?*
>
> Earth now
>
> On the busy brow.
>
> > *And where is the voice that I heard crying?"*

[*Exit Fidelio.*

SCENE 2

The court-room in the palace at Fiort, crowded with restless and expectant people. The crowd is arranged on both sides of the stage, in such a way that a broad avenue is left in the middle, leading from the footlights to the back of the stage and gradually narrowing to a point at Beatrice's throne. On the extreme right and left of the stage, along the back of the crowd, stands

the guard, a large body of armed soldiers, at attention,
in double row. On either side the throne stands an
armed soldier. As the curtain rises the court is all
standing and looking off stage in a certain direction.
Enter the Queen, Beatrice, from that direction, walks
in, looking straight ahead, goes to the throne and
seats herself. The court sits. The clerk begins to
read.

CLERK. The first case to be heard is that of Lisa,
    A widow with two small children, who resides
    Near the Duke's wood, and has been caught in the
        act
    Of cutting trees there, and hauling them home to
        burn.

BEATRICE. Stand, Lisa. You are a widow, I am told,
    With two small children.

LISA.   Ay, Your Majesty,
    Two little boys.

BEATRICE.   I know another widow, Lisa,
    With two small children, — but hers are little girls.
    Have you been cutting trees on the Duke's land?

LISA. No, Majesty. I could not cut a tree.
    I have no axe.

BEATRICE.   And are you strong enough

To break a tree with your hands?

LISA.   No, Majesty.

BEATRICE. I see. What do you do, then? There must be
Some reason for this plaint.

LISA.   I gather wood
That's dead, — dried boughs, and underbrush that's been
A long time on the ground, and drag it home.

BEATRICE. Have you a woodpile?

LISA.   Nay. I gather enough
Each day for the day's need. I have no time
To gather more.

BEATRICE.   And does the dry wood burn
As well as other wood?

LISA.   Oh, better!

BEATRICE.   I see.
You would as lief, then, have this wood you gather,
This dead wood, as a green tree freshly cut?

LISA. Ay, I would liefer have it, Majesty.
I need a fire quickly. I have no time
To wait for wood to season.

BEATRICE.   You may sit down,
Lisa. Is the Duke's agent here?

AGENT. Ay, here.

BEATRICE. What is it the Duke's custom to have done
With this dead wood on his estate?

AGENT. He burns it,
Your Majesty.

BEATRICE. You mean to say, I think,
He pays a price to have it gathered and burned.

AGENT. Ay, Majesty.

BEATRICE. Where is it burned?

AGENT. In a clearing.

BEATRICE. And what is cooked upon it?

AGENT. Nothing is cooked.
The Duke is not a gypsy.
[*With irritation.*
*Pause. Slight titter in court-room, instantly hushed
into profound silence.*

BEATRICE (*evenly*). If he were,
He would be shrewder, and not be paying money
For what this woman is glad to do for naught.
Nothing is cooked, and nobody is warmed, —
A most unthrifty fire. Do you bid the Duke,
Until he show me sounder cause for plaint,
Permit this woman to gather unmolested
Dead wood in his forest, and bear it home. — Lisa,

Take care you break no half-green boughs. The
next case?

CLERK. Is that of Mario, a miller, accused
Of stealing grain. A baker, by name Pietro,
Brings this complaint against him.

MESSENGER (*rushing in and up to throne*). Majesty,
Bianca of Lagoverde lies a-dying,
And calls for you!

BEATRICE (*rising*).   She calls for me?

MESSENGER.   Ay, Majesty.
[*Beatrice stands very still a moment, then turns to
the townspeople.*

BEATRICE (*earnestly and rapidly*). You people, do
you go now and live kindly
Till I return. I may not stay to judge you;
Wherefore I set you free. For I would rather
A knave should go at large than that a just man
Be punished. If there be a knave among you,
Let him live thoughtfully till I return.
(*She steps down from the throne, and is imme-
diately seized by the arm on either side by the two
guards who have been standing beside the throne*)
Why, what is this, Enrico?
(*Looking up at the soldier on her right*)

Nay, it is not

Enrico! (*Looking to other side*) Nor is it Pablo!
  How is this?

(*From each side of the stage one row of the double
row of soldiers detaches itself, marches down around
the front of the stage and up towards the throne,
making an armed alley for the Queen to walk down,
and entirely surrounding the crowd*)

Nay, all new faces. So! Upon my word,
This is a marvelous sight. — Do you stand back
And keep your fingers from me! — I see you there,
Angelo! Do not turn your head aside!
And you, Filippo! — Is the sick hand better
I bound the bandage on? — Is't well enough
To draw a sword against me? — Nay, I am sick.
I, that have loved you as your mothers love you —
And you do this to me! Lead me away.

[*The two guards lead out the Queen. Nobody else
moves. The townspeople cower and stare. The two
little pages that bore her train as she entered remain
back of the throne, not knowing what to do. As she
goes by them, her train dragging on the ground, the
two ragged little boys of Lisa, the wood-gatherer,*

run out from the group of citizens, pick up the ends
of the train, and go out, holding it up, one of them
with his arm over his eyes.

Scene 3

A dungeon. Beatrice alone, sitting on a bench, her
head bowed in her hands. Enter Guido.

BEATRICE. Guido, is't you!

GUIDO.   Ay, it is I, my Queen.
You sent for me, an I mistake not?

BEATRICE.   Ay.
Guido, you will not keep me when I tell you
Snow-White is dying and calls my name!

GUIDO.   I knew that.

BEATRICE. You knew that, and you hold me here. Oh,
Heaven!
What are you?

GUIDO.   I am a man. You should have thought
Of that before. I could have been your friend
If it had pleased you. Failing that, I am
Your enemy. I am too aware of you,
And have been ever, to hold me in at less.

BEATRICE. Guido. I beg of you upon my knees
　　To let me go!

GUIDO. 　　　　　　And why should I do that?

BEATRICE. For pity's sake!

GUIDO. 　　　　　　　I do not know the word.

BEATRICE. Then for the sake of my sworn hand and
　　seal
　　Upon a paper yielding fair to you
　　This sovereignty you prize. It is to me
　　Little enough to-night. I give it gladly.

GUIDO. You have no power to give what I have
　　taken
　　Already, and hold upon my hand, Rose-Red.

BEATRICE. Oh, do not speak that name! Oh, Guido,
　　Guido,
　　I cannot suffer further! Let me go!
　　If only for a moment, let me go!
　　I will return, — I will but take her hand,
　　And come away! I swear it! Let me go!

GUIDO. On one condition only.

BEATRICE. 　　　　　　　Ay. 'Tis granted,
　　Ere it is spoken!

GUIDO. 　　　　That upon returning
　　You come to me, and give yourself to me,

To lie in my arms lovingly.   (*She is stricken speech-*
less) You hear?

To lie in my arms lovingly.

BEATRICE.   Oh, God!

GUIDO. It is my only word.

BEATRICE.   Oh, God! Oh, God!

GUIDO. 'Tis granted?

BEATRICE.   Nay, — I cannot! I will die
Instead. Oh, God, to think that she will lie
there
And call for me, and I will never come!

GUIDO. Good night.

[*He goes to door.*

BEATRICE (*in a quiet voice*). Guido!

It shall be as you say.

GUIDO (*rushing to her*). Ah, Beatrice!

BEATRICE.   Nay, touch me not yet.

I will return.   (*She laughs like a child*) Why, 'tis a
simple matter!

I wonder now that even for a moment
I held myself so dear! When for her sake
All things are little things! — This foolish body,
This body is not I! There is no I,
Saving the need I have to go to her!

SCENE 4

A room at Lagoverde. Bianca lying in bed, ill to death. The children clinging to the bed, their nurse trying to draw them away. Giulietta, a maid, in the background. Possibly other attendants about.

LITTLE ROSE-RED. Finish the story, mother!

NURSE. Come away, now!

LITTLE SNOW-WHITE. Finish the story!

BIANCA. Do you go away with nurse
A little while. You will bring them back to me
Later?

NURSE (*weeping*). Ay, madam.

[*She goes out with the children.*

BIANCA. Later — not much later,
I think. — Hear you no sound of horses yet,
Giulietta, galloping this way?

GIULIETTA. Nay, not yet.

BIANCA (*to herself*). I will not go until she comes. I
will not.
Still, — if I should — Giulietta!

GIULIETTA (*coming quickly to the bed*). Ay, my
mistress!

BIANCA. She will come, I tell you!

GIULIETTA.   Ay, I doubt it not.

BIANCA. Ay, she will come. But if she should come
    late,

And I no longer be here to receive her,

Show her all courtesy, I conjure you.

She will be weary, and mightily distraught.

Make her take wine, — and bring the children to
    her.

And tell her, they are hers now. She is their mother.

(*Giulietta starts to go back to the window*)

And say to her — wait! — I have a message for her.

Say to her this, Giulietta: The foot stumbles,

The hand hath its own awkward way; the tongue

Moves foolishly in the mouth; but in the heart

The truth lies, — and all's well 'twixt her and me.

Can you remember that?

GIULIETTA.   Ay, madam, I think so.

If not the words, at least the gist of it.

BIANCA. Forget it all, my good child, but forget not:

All's well 'twixt her and me.

GIULIETTA.   Nay, that I have.

BIANCA. I will sleep now a little. Do you leave me.

But go not far. (*She lies still for a moment, then
    starts up*)

I hear the sound of hoof-beats!

GIULIETTA. Nay, madam.

BIANCA.   Ay, I tell you! I can hear them!
My face upon the pillow brings my ear
Nearer the ground! She is coming! Open the door!
[*She kneels up in bed and holds out her arms towards the door, maintaining this position till Beatrice comes. Giulietta, weeping, opens the door, and stands in it, shaking her head sadly.*

GIULIETTA (*suddenly lifting her head and listening*).
Nay, it is so! I hear it now myself!
Ay, there's a horse upon the bridge!

BIANCA.   She's coming!
Stand back! Stand out of the doorway!
[*Pause.*

SERVANT (*entering*).   Majesty,
The Queen is here.

BIANCA.   Ay, ay! Stand out of the doorway!
[*Pause.*

GIULIETTA. She is here! She is in the court! She has
   leapt from horse!
Madam, Oh, God be praised! This way!

BIANCA.   Sister!
[*Beatrice enters in her riding clothes, leaps to the*

*bed. Bianca throws her arms about her neck, and
dies.*

BEATRICE (*after a moment, looking down at her*).
Snow-White! Oh, no!

Oh, no! Snow-White! (*She screams*) Ah-h!
Help me!

She is dying!

[*Attendants and nurses rush in, also the children.*

LITTLE SNOW-WHITE. Mother, wake up!

LITTLE ROSE-RED. Finish the story!

BEATRICE. Take them away. Snow-White!

[*Leaning over the bed.*

NURSE. Nay, it is over,
Madam.

BEATRICE. Leave me. Leave me alone with her.

[*Exeunt all but Beatrice. She kneels beside the bed.*

SCENE 5

*A room at Lagoverde. The next day. Beatrice
alone.*

BEATRICE. In sooth, I do not feel the earth so firm
Under my feet as yesterday it was.

All that I loved have gone to a far land,

And left me here alone, save for two children
And twenty thousand enemies, and the thing
Of horror that's in store for me.   Almost
I feel my feet uprooted from the earth,
There's such a tugging at me to be gone.
Save for your children (*looking off stage towards
Bianca's room*), 'twould be simple enough
To lay me down beside you in your bed,
And call on Death, who is not yet out of hearing,
To take me, too.
[*Enter Fidelio.*

FIDELIO.   Mistress, I have news for you.
Guido is dead!
BEATRICE.   Is dead?
FIDELIO.   Ay, he is dead.
Dead of a dagger i' the back, — and dead enough
For twenty.   Scarce were you gone an hour's time
We came upon him cold.   And in a pool
Nearby, the Lady Francesca floating drowned,
Who last was seen a-listening like a ghost
At the door of the dungeon.   'Tis a marvelous
    thing!
But that's not all!
BEATRICE.   Nay, what more can there be?

FIDELIO.   Mistress, in the night the people of Fiori
Rose like a wind and swept the Duke's men down
Like leaves! Come home! Come home! We will
have supper
On a flat rock, behind a mulberry bush,
Of milk and tarts and honey and white bread —
All in one day!

BEATRICE.   There is but half of me
To hear your tidings. I would clap my hands to-
gether
But one of them is stricken from my side.
[Enter Giulietta.

GIULIETTA.   Madam.

BEATRICE.   Ay, Giulietta.

GIULIETTA.   Madam, last night,
Before you came, she bade me tell you something,
And not forget. 'Tis this: That the foot stumbles,
The hand doth awkward things, and the foolish
tongue
Says what it would not say, — but in the heart
Truth lies, — and all is well 'twixt her and you.
(She starts to go out, and turns back at the door)
She bade me above all things to forget not

The last: that all is well 'twixt her and you.
[*Exit.*

BEATRICE (*slowly and with great content*).
She is not gone from me. Oh, there be places
Farther away than Death! She is returned
From her long silence, and rings out above me
Like a silver bell! — Let us go back, Fidelio,
And gather up the fallen stones, and build us
Another tower.

CURTAIN